From Tragic to Magic

This engaging and colourful story and guide has been created to prepare children for reading and spelling through the recognition of phonological patterns such as rhyme, syllables and the awareness of phonemes within words. By working on and strengthening language skills, in turn, you are building children's literacy abilities – together.

A prequel to the storybook, *Who Put the Spell into Spelling?*, *From Tragic to Magic* tells the story of three siblings who set out to rescue their teacher, Miss Tragic. As they battle with a giant, a witch and a wizard, they encounter three phonological challenges that focus on syllables, rhyming and phonemes.

Key features include:

- Games and prompt questions for each chapter, based on Bloom's Taxonomy, to assess memory, understanding, application, analysis, evaluation and creativity
- A selection of additional activities to help to continue developing phonological awareness beyond the story
- Guidance and support for the adult reader throughout

With beautiful accompanying illustrations, this fun fairy tale provides an exciting and imaginative way of preparing children up to 7 years old for phonics, reading and spelling at primary school. It is an essential resource for parents, carers, grandparents and early educators.

Georgie Cooney works for the Dyslexia Association of Ireland (DAI) and teaches students with Specific Learning Difficulties (SpLDs). She first worked as a classroom teacher both in the UK and in the USA, and then re-trained in the field of language and literacy. After becoming a dyslexia specialist, she has lectured, trained teachers, managed and coordinated Inclusion and Special Educational Needs in both mainstream and specialist settings. Georgie is also the author of *Who Put the Spell into Spelling?* – a beautifully illustrated storybook and workbook set designed to help children remember and use spelling rules. She seeks to improve the literacy skills of all children and adults, in the hope that this will widen their opportunities in life.

From Tragic to Magic: A Phonological Fairy Tale and Guide to Prepare Children for Literacy

Written by **Georgie Cooney**

Illustrated by **Molly Hickey**

Routledge
Taylor & Francis Group

LONDON AND NEW YORK

First published 2021
by Routledge
2 Park Square, Milton Park, Abingdon, Oxon OX14 4RN

and by Routledge
605 Third Avenue, New York, NY 10158

Routledge is an imprint of the Taylor & Francis Group, an informa business

British Library Cataloguing-in-Publication Data
A catalogue record for this book is available from the British Library

Library of Congress Cataloging-in-Publication Data
Names: Cooney, Georgie, author. | Hickey, Molly, illustrator.
Title: From tragic to magic: a phonological fairy tale and guide to
prepare children for literacy / Georgie Cooney; illustrated by Molly Hickey.
Description: Abingdon, Oxon; New York, NY: Routledge, 2021.
Identifiers: LCCN 2020052439 (print) | LCCN 2020052440 (ebook) |
ISBN 9780367708610 (hardback) | ISBN 9780367685928 (paperback) |
ISBN 9781003138211 (ebook)
Subjects: LCSH: Reading–Phonetic method. |
Reading (Early childhood) | Reading (Elementary)
Classification: LCC LB1573.3 .C66 2021 (print) |
LCC LB1573.3 (ebook) | DDC 372.46/5–dc23
LC record available at https://lccn.loc.gov/2020052439
LC ebook record available at https://lccn.loc.gov/2020052440

ISBN: 978-0-367-70861-0 (hbk)
ISBN: 978-0-367-68592-8 (pbk)
ISBN: 978-1-003-13821-1 (ebk)

Typeset in Avenir and VAG Rounded
by Newgen Publishing UK

Dedication

This is dedicated to our beautiful cousin Kate Batt. She was such a kind and thoughtful cousin, a stalwart for many. Her legacy lives on in her husband Charles and her children, Rosie and George. She was a true and wonderful member of the Kinds (as explained later in the book).

We also dedicate this to Molly's great-aunt Mary-Rose, who is also my mum. Mum clearly had very strong foundations in language because her literacy skills are incredible. She has guided this book and helped to develop the characters, first created by my adorable dad. Thank you to my wise and clever mum, you are a literacy superstar.

Contents

Acknowledgements viii

Introduction 1

Chapter 1 – Miss Tragic 5

Syllables 11

Chapter 2 – Ginormous the Giant and Syllables 12

Rhyme 19

Chapter 3 – Esmerelda the Witch and Rhymes 20

Phonemes 27

Chapter 4 – Wisdom the Wizard and Phonemes 29

Phonological Awareness Games and Activities 40

Phoneme Table 46

Acknowledgements

Molly and I were lucky to have parents who read to us at home. We know that we were very fortunate and that there are many children who are less fortunate. When it was mum's turn to read to my siblings and me, we heard about the travels of Babar and Celeste, the magical adventures of Mumfie the Elephant and about weird and wonderful characters such as Mrs Pepperpot. When it was dad's turn to read, he didn't. Instead, he told us the stories of Esmerelda the Witch, Wisdom the Wizard and Ginormous the Giant. They were always up to no good and the three siblings – Anne, Andrew and Angela – were generally involved with some misdemeanour involving super glue. Clearly my characters have been drawn from these – with such very fond memories.

I also want to thank friends and colleagues such as Margaret Bevan, Val Hammond, Christine Kelly, Alex Mackichan-Burke and Ella Burns who all share the same passion for trying to help young children with their language and their literacy skills. There are many educators, parents and carers out there, desperately trying to equip children and young people to strengthen their language skills and, in turn, literacy skills too. Bella Northey and Brett Tyne must also get a mention for their kind listening ears and editing eyes.

Introduction

This illustrated book has been created for you to prepare your children for literacy and to explore the very important foundations of language with them. Whether you're a parent, carer or teacher, helping your child's language skills will give them a better chance to prepare well for literacy. If they have strong language, they are more likely to have strong literacy. If they have strong literacy skills, then their life opportunities are likely to be stronger and better.

It may be that your child is already learning literacy skills at school, but you have identified that they are lacking understanding in some basic language abilities. Or it may be the case that they are struggling to acquire phonics or sight words. This book can also be used interactively, alongside the acquisition of literacy skills, but the sooner their language knowledge is strengthened, the better position they are in to learn to read and write.

You and your child will be taken on a beautifully illustrated journey to try and find their teacher who has been kidnapped. You will be challenged at three language levels and together you will rescue her.

The language skills you will practise in this story are based on phonological awareness:

1. Syllables (Chapter 2)
2. Rhyme (Chapter 3)
3. **Phonemes** (Chapter 4)

Having good phonological awareness as a learner means that you are more likely to use that awareness to tackle literacy demands in reading and spelling.

What is phonological awareness?

It is the ability to recognise (hear) and use sounds in spoken language.

I personally think that there are three main stages of phonological awareness that can be split into sub skills:

1. Syllables
   a) being able to **blend** syllables
   b) being able to **segment** syllables
2. Rhyme
   a) being able to **detect** rhyme
   b) being able to **generate** rhyme
3. **Phonemes**
   a) hearing that words can start with the same sound (**alliteration**)
      e.g. **S**am's smelly socks stink!
   b) being able to blend individual letter sounds (**blending**)
      e.g. /c/ /a/ /t/ = 'cat'
   c) being able to segment individual letter sounds (**segmenting**)
      e.g. 'chat' = /ch/ /a/ /t/
   d) being able to manipulate sounds (**sound manipulation**)
      e.g. 'fish' with a /d/ is 'dish' or 'fish' with /g/ at the end is 'fig'.

How is this fairy tale phonological?

This phonological fairy tale is based on language skills involving **listening and speaking** only. There is no reading or writing required because these phonological skills need to be in place before the children move on to read and spell phonics and sight words.

When a child starts school, they will be required to begin reading and writing. So, by reading this and working with them on these challenges, you will be doing everything you can to get them ready for literacy.

Why is phonological awareness so important?

Learning to read and spell tends to develop in accumulative stages – it is a process. The development of one stage, leads to the development of the next stage.

1. Phonological Awareness

2. Phonics

3. Vocabulary Development

4. Reading Fluency

5. Reading Comprehension

It is evident from research that children who start school with a strong foundation of phonological awareness learn to read faster and with more ease than their peers. It is also well known that many literacy difficulties are identified because of, amongst other things, an individual's poor phonological awareness. Dyslexia is well known and one of these specific literacy difficulties.

If this book focuses on language, how does it help them with literacy skills?

Through practising these activities, children will start to recognise sound patterns which they will also see in both reading and writing. These patterns could be in the form of syllables, rhyme or **phonemes** (which the children later relate to graphemes).

You will be introduced to each part of phonological awareness at the beginning of each chapter and have plenty of opportunities to practise the parts throughout the story and with the activities at the end of the book.

You will see that you can take breaks in the story to play games and activities which, in turn, will help your children to empathise with the characters and progress their own language abilities. There is no time limit with this book. Take as long as you need. As we know, every child is a different learner – there is no one size that fits all.

Questions

There are a series of questions in each chapter. These are based on Bloom's Taxonomy of questions with a hierarchy of levels in order to challenge your child to think just beyond remembering the basics. The questions are a guide to help them learn the necessary information for becoming independent thinkers and problem solvers.

Initially, some of the questions might be too challenging because your child isn't ready for them yet. That is completely fine, so don't ask them the questions if that is the case. Maybe come back to them at a later time when they feel more confident with the task you're working on. If a child has a diagnosed Speech, Language and Communication Need (SLCN) then it may be that there are some questions that are beyond their means (at the time) and, as adults, we need to be mindful of this. Just do your utmost to ensure they have the basic concept. You know the child best so please think carefully about how far they can be challenged. Remember that our aim is to increase their confidence in their own language ability. We want them to feel well equipped for learning literacy.

I really hope that you have fun with your child whilst reading this story and that you both enjoy strengthening your language skills throughout the activities. You can play so many games both with the story and after you have finished the book; play them on car journeys, whilst out shopping, at school and at home on an everyday basis.

How to read this book

This is entirely up to you but there is a benefit in reading through the whole story first in order to get the general understanding and hear the key words. Check your child's understanding by asking them a few comprehension questions at the end. Then, go back to the beginning and start again, this time playing the games and asking some of the set questions. There is no one way of doing this. Pick and choose activities that your child needs or do all of them!

Obviously, there are directions for the adults and these are identified by a finger pointed towards you, the adult:

When it is time to 'read together', you will see this picture:

Please enjoy!

Chapter 1: Miss Tragic

We start our story in a land that is similar to where you live but this land has more hills, trees, mountains, rivers and seas than you'll ever know. It is known as Phon. This is a Greek word meaning 'sound'. Sound can have highs and lows, like mountains and valleys and rollercoasters. Human beings can also have highs and lows, like waves.

As with most lands, Phon has goodness and badness. The nice folk are known as **Kinds**. They tend to care for others and have big, open minds about their land and the world in which their land exists.

The not-so-nice chaps are known as the Selfish. They're more 'sel' than 'fish'. They don't have anything to do with fish, they tend to just do things for themselves. So, in fact, let's just call them 'Selves'. This works because there are many elves in the gang of Selves. Anyway, back to the story …

Three siblings Anita, Andreas and Angelica are sitting at home because their school is closed. Their teacher, Miss Tragic, has gone missing! Miss Tragic is a particularly lovely **Kind** but everything seems to be going wrong for her at the moment.

No one knows where she has gone but …

Anita (who is bold and brave) is determined to find out. Andreas (who is curious and clever) thinks he knows how to find Miss Tragic. Angelica (who is kind and cute) thinks that she is going to cry. Angelica is always crying.

To stop Angelica from crying, Anita decides that they're all going to go and find Miss Tragic.

Andreas (who loves to solve problems) has finished his thought process and thinks he has the answer:

'I bet those Selves who live in the Tall Towering Tower: Ginormous the Giant, Esmerelda the Witch and **Wisdom the Wizard** have kidnapped Miss Tragic!'

'Why do you think that?' asks Anita.

'I heard that some of the Selves were trying to find a teacher to teach them new spells, but no one would educate them because they're all too mean. So, they have kidnapped Miss Tragic in the hope that she will teach them new spells', Andreas explains with great satisfaction.

'Right then, let's go and find her in the Tall Towering Tower', insists Anita.

'Oh no, I don't want to go, I'm scared', Angelica whimpers.

'Such a cry baby Angelica! Come on, we're going!' commands Anita. With that, she pushes them all out of the door, on the hunt for the Tall Towering Tower.

The three children walk and walk and walk until they see the Tall Towering Tower in the distance.

Questions

You only need to ask as many questions as you think the child might answer.

Level 1. Remember: Where are these children living?

(Answer: Land of Phon.)

Level 2. Understand: Can you explain what happened to Miss Tragic?

(Answer: They think she has been kidnapped by some Selves: Ginormous the Giant, Esmerelda the Witch, and Wisdom the Wizard.)

Level 3. Can apply: What would you have done in the same situation?

(Answer: Any.)

Level 4. Can analyse: What are the differences between the three siblings?

(Answer: Angelica is strong, bossy, decisive etc. Andreas is clever, smart, a thinker etc. Angelica is young, scared, cry-baby, sweet natured etc.)

Level 5. Can evaluate: Do you think it would it be better if the children stayed at home?

(Answer: Any.)

Level 6. Can create: If you could create your own land – would you have good and bad creatures or people living there?

(Answer: Any.)

Syllables

In this chapter, you are introduced to
Ginormous the Giant **who speaks in** syllables.

Syllables are beats in words.

Every single syllable has to have a VOWEL SOUND in it.

- The vowels are the sounds for a-e-i-o-u and 'y' can act as a vowel or a consonant.
- 'y' can sound like 'i's name in words such as 'my', 'fly', 'cry'.
- 'y' can also sound like 'e's name in words such as 'an-gry' or 'happ-y'.
- 'r' and 'w' can modify a vowel sound e.g. 'war', 'wand', 'sort', 'skirt'.

Your child needs to be able to **blend** syllables in order to be able to **segment** syllables e.g. the segmented win-dow, if **blended**, becomes the word 'window'; or the word 'elephant' can be **segmented** into three syllables /el/ /eph/ /ant/.

You will find that in this chapter you will play with syllables. Here are some activities you can play to practise syllables *(see the Phonological Awareness Games on pages 40–41 for more details on how to play the games)*:

- Robot Speaking
- Tapping/Clapping/Drumming
- Syllable Ping-Pong
- Syllable Picture Cues
- Pushing Forward
- Identifying Specific Syllables
- Syllable Bingo; Syllable Snap; Syllable Charades

Chapter 2: Ginormous the Giant and Syllables

 When Ginormous the Giant speaks – you need to speak slowly and in *syll-ab-les* (remember that *syllables* are beats in words).

I have broken the words up for you.

 The siblings finally reach the Tall Towering Tower and they knock on the enormous door.

To their surprise, Ginormous the Giant opens the door.

'I am Gi-nor-mous the Gi-ant. What do you three young nui-san-ces want?'

'Excuse me, we have come here to collect Miss Tragic', says Anita confidently.

Ginormous the Giant grunts in his very slow, deep voice. 'Ho Ho Ho. You have to climb all the way up to the top of the tow-er if you want to find her. I can't let you go to the next floor un-less you solve my syll-ab-les'.

Amidst her tears, Angelica asks, 'Excuse me Ginormous, what are syll-ab-les?'

'WHAT?' roars the giant.

'Oh no, sorry giant, Angelica is a bit upset. Of course she knows what syllables are' Andreas swiftly interrupts. 'Syllables are beats in words and they must contain a vowel sound!'

The giant looks happier with this answer.

'I will let you in if you solve my syll-ab-les' says the giant, extremely slowly.

'Which of you re-volt-ing child-ren is the old-est?'

'I am!' Anita cries with gusto. 'Fire away you Ginormous Giant you!'

The giant scratches his chin and thinks for a very long time. Eventually he asks:

'What am I say-ing?'

'Saying!' shouts Anita.

'Ey?...No!...You did not let me fin-ish' the giant roars. 'What am I say-ing now? … cu-cum-ber' he finally reveals.

'Easy! You said 'cucumber', which I hate by the way', Anita exclaims. She starts to walk towards the door leading into the tower to make her way to the next floor but the Giant yells 'WAIT! I have not fin-ished yet, young la-dy'.

Anita rolls her eyes.

'Now you have to tell me how ma-ny syll-ab-les are in the next three words:

Sau-sa-ges

Hel-ic-op-ters

Hipp-o-pot-am-us'

Ginormous is looking quite smug. He doesn't think Anita can get these.

Anita uses buttons on her coat to help her count:

'Sau-sa-ges – three; hel-ic-op-ters – four; and hipp-o-pot-a-mus – five!' Anita smiles as she finishes.

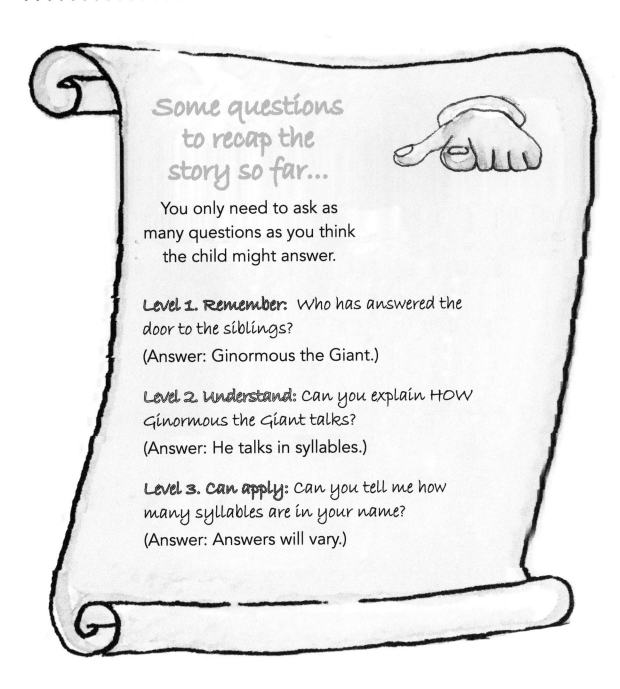

Some questions to recap the story so far...

You only need to ask as many questions as you think the child might answer.

Level 1. Remember: Who has answered the door to the siblings?
(Answer: Ginormous the Giant.)

Level 2. Understand: Can you explain HOW Ginormous the Giant talks?
(Answer: He talks in syllables.)

Level 3. Can apply: Can you tell me how many syllables are in your name?
(Answer: Answers will vary.)

Ginormous is not happy. He begrudgingly opens the door and lets her through. He then turns to Andreas who is practising his syllables under his breath and Angelica who is still tearful.

'Now for you two litt-le squidg-es...'

Let's now pretend that we are Angelica and Andreas and show that giant how smart we are with our syllables!

Syllable practice

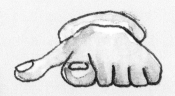

If your children need help counting the syllables, use counting aids such as counters, pens, pencils or buttons and push them forward for each syllable that they say so that they can go back and count them.

Questions for Andreas

Question one:

What is this word? Pen-cil (pencil)

Question two:

How many syllables in the next three words?

Wizardry (Answer: 3)

Frogs (Answer: 1)

Giants (Answer: 2)

Questions for Angelica

Question one:

What is this word? Wiz-ard (wizard)

Question two:

How many syllables in the next three words?

Mouse (Answer: 1)

Hurricane (Answer: 3)

Pirates (Answer: 2)

Ginormous is looking very worried. 'Oh dear – you have done quite a good job, so go and join your sis-ter up-stairs. Es-mer-el-da and Wis-dom are go-ing to make my life mis-er-ab-le'.

Ginormous, looking defeated, sits in a heap in a very large chair and sulks.

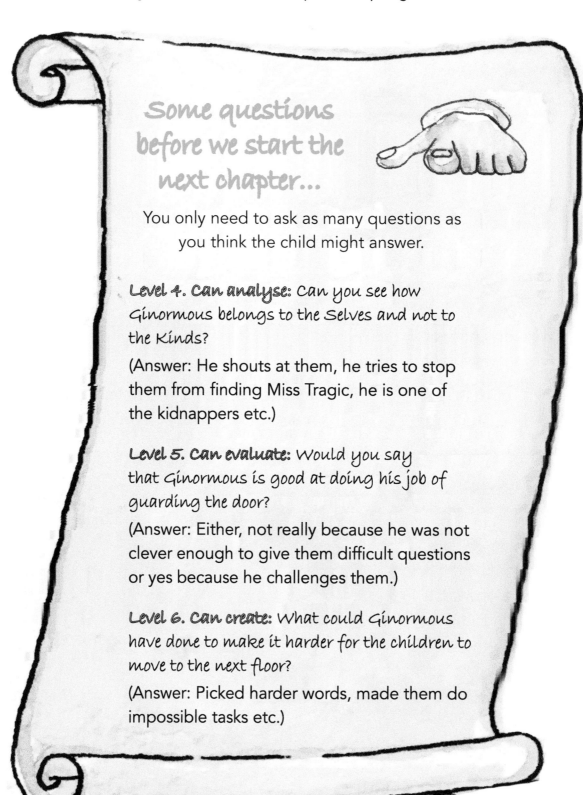

Some questions before we start the next chapter...

You only need to ask as many questions as you think the child might answer.

Level 4. Can analyse: Can you see how Ginormous belongs to the Selves and not to the Kinds?
(Answer: He shouts at them, he tries to stop them from finding Miss Tragic, he is one of the kidnappers etc.)

Level 5. Can evaluate: Would you say that Ginormous is good at doing his job of guarding the door?
(Answer: Either, not really because he was not clever enough to give them difficult questions or yes because he challenges them.)

Level 6. Can create: What could Ginormous have done to make it harder for the children to move to the next floor?
(Answer: Picked harder words, made them do impossible tasks etc.)

Rhyme

In this chapter, Esmerelda the Witch **speaks in** rhyme **and casts a spell in** rhyme.

Rhyme is a sequence of words (often found in poems or verse) where there are similar sounds, especially **end** sounds in words e.g. fat, cat, sat mat, hat, chat, spat etc. are all part of the /at/ rime family.

'Onset and rime' is the term used to explain words that rhyme but start with a different sound e.g. **c**+at (cat), **h**+at (hat), **m**+at (mat), **gn**+at (gnat), **ch**+at, **sp**+at. They all have a different onset.

It is really important to the development of a child's sound awareness that they can identify rhyme in words. If they can identify or detect rhyme then they can go on to generate their own rhymes. They will also be able to recognise words that share the same rime or word family e.g. pill, hill, spill, chill, frill, grill, thrill etc. If they can recognise these words and remember their word families then they will have more success spelling the words too.

There are many rhyming activities. Start with practising rhyme detection (hearing the rhyme) and move on to rhyme generation (producing rhyme). Together, you could even come up with your own nursery rhymes or raps. Visual cues (such as picture cards) really help with rhyming games and the games can be made harder if you take the visuals away – the children will have to rely more heavily on memory recall. Activities you can play to practise rhyme *(see the Phonological Awareness Games on pages 41–42 for more details on how to play the games)*:

Rhyme detection:

- Rhyming Pelmanism
- Rhyming Snap
- Picture and Word
- Feely Bag or Box
- Odd One Out
- Rhyming Bingo

Rhyme generating:

- Turn-Taking Game
- Rhyming Cards
- I Spy with Semantic Clues
- Feely Bag
- Rhyming Couplets

Chapter 3: Esmerelda the Witch and Rhymes

The children work their way up a dark, narrow, winding staircase. It seems to go on and on and on until they reach a large door. It is smaller than the last one but this one has a strange cat's face on the front. It is a doorknocker but the eyes appear to be moving, which even scares Anita a little bit. Just as she raises her hand to knock, the witch's face suddenly appears!

'Hello little children' says the witch with a nasty, nasal noise.

'I am Esmerelda and I speak in rhyme.

If you want to enter, you might possibly in time.

I suspect you won't though,

As you're several levels below

The intelligence I show'.

'Excuse me!' exclaimed Anita, stunned at the rudeness of the witch.

'We are actually really clever.

We seriously endeavour

To find Miss Tragic

And end you selfish people forever!'

The door swings open beyond Esmerelda's control because Anita has spoken in rhyme! The witch is very shocked but soon remembers that she is still a witch with greater powers than they have.

'Oh you think you're so clever,

Well try to work this spell out,

Because you won't ever!'

The witch laughs a nasty,
cackling laugh.

Esmerelda's Spell

Hocus, pocus, twiddly doo,

I am going to put a spell on you

I'll turn you all into ugly swine

*Unless you can find a
perfect rhyme*

*That easily matches this one
of mine*

You'll stay like that forever in time!

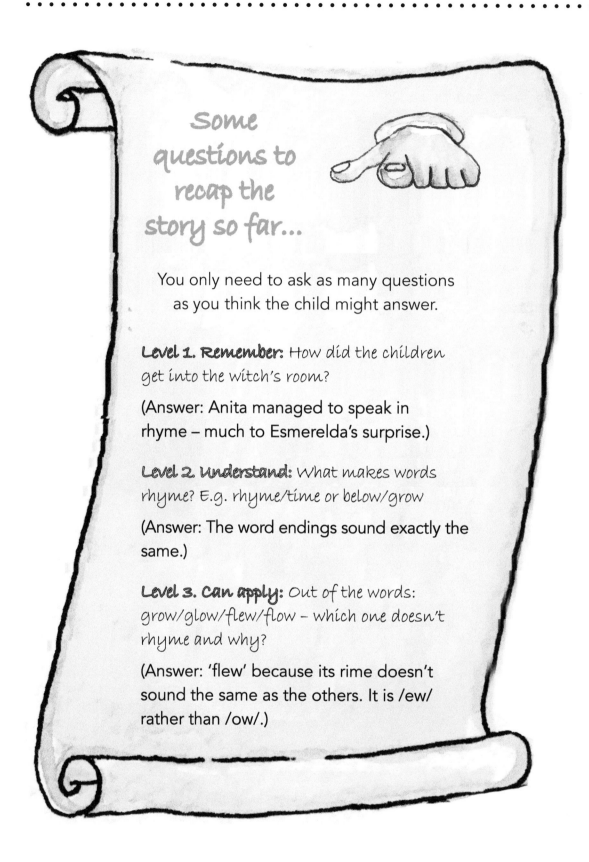

Some questions to recap the story so far...

You only need to ask as many questions as you think the child might answer.

Level 1. Remember: How did the children get into the witch's room?

(Answer: Anita managed to speak in rhyme – much to Esmerelda's surprise.)

Level 2. Understand: What makes words rhyme? E.g. rhyme/time or below/grow

(Answer: The word endings sound exactly the same.)

Level 3. Can apply: Out of the words: grow/glow/flew/flow – which one doesn't rhyme and why?

(Answer: 'flew' because its rime doesn't sound the same as the others. It is /ew/ rather than /ow/.)

The children have been taught how to rhyme in school, so they just need to think of words that sound the same as Esmerelda's. Andreas cleverly recorded the witch when she created the spell so they can hear it on his phone. He presses play:

Anita, Andreas and Angelica are going to find rhyming words to try and create a better spell than the witch's. Can you help them find more words to rhyme with theirs?

'Hocus, pocus, twiddly doo,

I am going to put a spell on you.

Angelica points out that 'doo and you' rhyme so they then find rhyming words: pooh, moo, loo, grew, flew, true, who, blue, due.

I'll turn you all into ugly swine

Anita knows that fine, line, dine, sign, mine, twine all rhyme with swine.

Unless you can find a perfect rhyme

That easily matches this one of mine

You'll stay like that forever in time!

So 'swine' and 'mine' rhyme and 'rhyme' and 'time' rhyme so they find the following rhyming words for rhyme and time: chime, climb, lime, dime, slime, prime, grime, anytime, summertime, wintertime etc.

With all of these amazing words they have collected, they come up with the perfect spell!

'You asked us to find a spell

That rhymes with yours...

We think you smell,

So, let's open some doors.

The witch looks annoyed but the children giggle. Then together they rhyme:

Hocus, pocus, twiddly pooh,

We have a spell to put on you.

We'll send you to the deepest mine

And turn you into a pool of slime

No sun there will ever shine

And you will stay forever in stinky grime!

At which point, the witch disappears in a flash! All the children can see is a pool of slime slowly oozing down the outside of the tower and disappearing into the ground. The children can't help but laugh and clap.

If you're having any problems hearing the rhymes or coming up with your own, don't forget that there are loads of rhyming games that you can play at the back of the book.

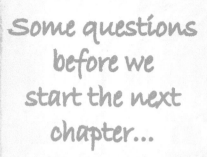

Some questions before we start the next chapter...

You only need to ask as many questions as you think the child might answer.

Level 4. Can analyse: How does the children's spell compare with Esmerelda's spell?

(Answer: The children find a better spell that gets rid of the witch forever!).

Level 5. Can evaluate: How would you feel if the witch had put a spell on you?

(Answers will vary.)

Level 6. Can create: Could you come up with a better rhyming spell?

(Have a go and let's see what the witch turns into... .)

Phonemes

In this chapter, Wisdom the Wizard **uses a more advanced trickery with language. He plays games with** phonemes. **These are units of sounds that can be used to make words that children recognise.**

You can <u>hear</u> them but you can't read them or write them without learning the graphemes (the written representation). An example of this is the /ch/ phoneme in the word 'child', that is written as the grapheme: 'c' and 'h' together. (A complete table of phonemes can be found at the back of the book.)

A learner can accumulate phonemes in stages so that they can eventually manipulate them to have a really good knowledge of the structure of words.

1. **Alliteration:** the occurrence of the same letter or sound at the beginning of adjacent or closely connected words e.g. **S**ally **s**ays **s**illy, **s**melly **s**ongs. Learners can play games like 'eye spy' and start to make connections.
2. **Phoneme blending:** blending phonemes together to create words e.g. the three phonemes /c/ /a/ /t/ make the word 'cat' or the four phonemes /b/ /l/ /a/ /ck/ make the word 'black'.
3. **Phoneme segmentation:** segmenting phonemes in words helps to hear how the word was built e.g. 'dog' can be segmented into /d/ /o/ /g/ – three phonemes. The word 'hatch' can also be segmented into three phonemes – /h/ /a/ /tch/. Yet the word 'skirt' has four phonemes /s/ /k/ /ir/ /t/.
4. **Phoneme deletion:** deleting a sound from a word can help a learner appreciate its structure e.g. 'fish' without /f/ is 'ish' but 'fish' without /sh/ is 'fi'; 'man' without /n/ is 'ma' and 'man' without /m/ is 'an'. Sometimes they start to hear how new words can be created.

5. **Phoneme substitution:** this is where sounds can be swapped and new words and sounds can be established e.g. with the word 'hat', I could swap the /a/ for an /i/ and have 'hit'. With the word 'cap', I could swap the /a/ with an /u/ and have 'cup'. With 'cap', I could also swap the /p/ for a /t/ and have 'cat' etc.

6. **Phoneme reversals (spoonerisms):** these are very advanced but prove the ability to manipulate sounds. You can swap the first sounds in **P**olly **H**unter and get **H**olly **P**unter or **K**ing **R**ichard can change to **R**ing **K**ichard.

Activities you can play to practise **phonemes** *(see the Phonological Awareness Games on pages 42–45 for more details on how to play the games)*:

- **Alliteration:** Feely Bag, Odd One Out, Turn-Taking, I Spy, I Went to the Market
- **Phoneme Blending:** Counters, Slow-Go, Uni-Fix Cubes, Instructions
- **Phoneme Segmentation:** Board Game, Counters or Cubes, Aim of the Game
- **Phoneme Deletion:** Elision Game, Counters or Cubes, What Do I Prefer?
- **Phoneme Substitution:** Guess What I Am Saying, Feely Bag, Picture Cards
- **Phoneme Reversals:** Well-Known People, Name Game, Compound Words

Chapter 4: Wisdom the Wizard and Phonemes

Anita, Andreas and Angelica creep their way up to the final door. They have to crawl as the space is getting smaller and the ceiling seems to be moving in closer to their heads. This final door is tiny. They might be able to squeeze through it if they're lucky.

They knock on the door and as it opens, a long, white beard tumbles out. **Wisdom the Wizard** is attached to the beard, but they can't see his face.

The siblings suddenly hear a rather high-pitched voice start to speak at great speed.

'Oh I don't know how you got up here but I am really rather annoyed. I have been having great fun dangling Miss Tragic off the top of the tower. The good news is that she is very light in weight. The bad news is that her name is so tragic that there really can only be terrible and tortuous tragedy ahead of her'.

'Uh well now Wisdom. You see, we have come to save her so, if you don't mind, we shall take her home with us', Anita says confidently.

'Oh you are quite a **f**unny, **f**rilly **f**illy! You seem terribly confident for a young **g**regarious, **g**orgeous **g**irl. I don't suppose you recognise how I talk do you? If you can't hear it, you definitely can't come in!'

'Yes, actually I know. You are using **alliteration** to describe Anita, which I can also do, you **w**eird, **w**ilful **w**izard', says Andreas intelligently.

Wisdom ignores Andreas and looks at Angelica.

'You look extremely **y**oung in **y**ears and **y**outhful. Your brother and sister might be able to do it but I bet you can't. If you can't then none of you can come in', says Wisdom as he laughs.

Angelica immediately feels like crying but she knows that they are so close to helping Miss Tragic that she swallows her tears and has a go …

'**W**isdom the **W**icked **W**izard!' There, she says it and all the words that matter, start with the same sound /**w**/.

Wisdom's white beard disappears and the door opens up to them. Now they see him. His nose is as pointy as his hat. He is not looking happy, but he rubs his hands together and starts to smile.

Wisdom starts to speak.

'Ok, you might have entered my **c**osy, **c**urvy **c**ave of a room but you still have to rescue Miss Tragic. I shall ask you a series of **q**ueer, **q**uirky **q**uestions and you have to get them all correct in order to get to the rooftop. Hah! This is hilarious! This will never happen! Right, the last to enter, must step forward'.

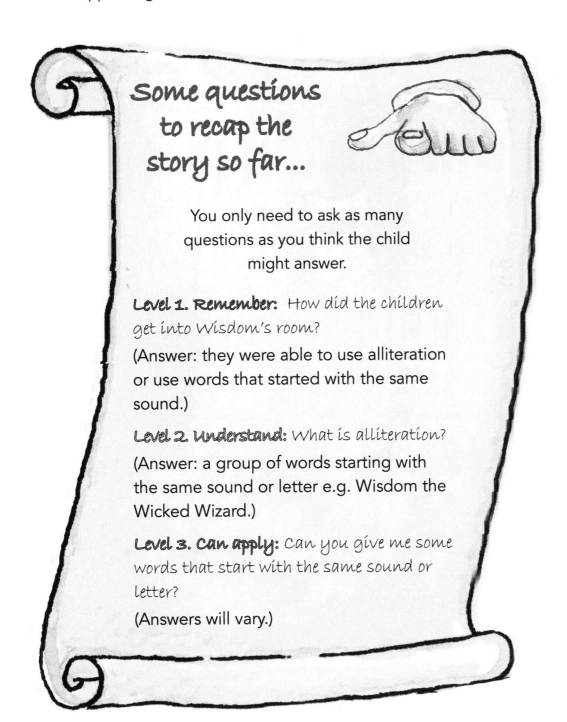

Some questions to recap the story so far...

You only need to ask as many questions as you think the child might answer.

Level 1. Remember: How did the children get into Wisdom's room?
(Answer: they were able to use alliteration or use words that started with the same sound.)

Level 2. Understand: What is alliteration?
(Answer: a group of words starting with the same sound or letter e.g. Wisdom the Wicked Wizard.)

Level 3. Can apply: Can you give me some words that start with the same sound or letter?
(Answers will vary.)

Angelica tiptoes towards him.

'How many letter sounds do you hear in the word…tragic?'

**Ask children to have a go at this and
try other words such as the names
of the characters in the story
e.g. Anita = 5 and Angelica = 8.**

Angelica has recently learnt her letter sounds in school so she feels brave enough
to say …

'/t/ /r/ /a/ /g/ /i/ /c/', using the buttons on Anita's coat, she counts and
shouts 'six!'

Wisdom, who is shocked, tries to not look bothered and turns to Andreas.

'If I take the /a/ sound away from Anita's name – what sound do I have left?'

Andreas is about to open his mouth to give him the answer, but then thinks a little
harder and sees that Wisdom is trying to trick him. Anita has two /a/ sounds in her
name: /a/ /n/ /i/ /t/ /a/.

Ask children to have a go at working this out. Do they hear the /nit/ when the /a/ is taken from the beginning and the end? Can you play with more words like this?

'Nit! Like the **n**asty **n**its living in your **w**hite, **w**ispy beard!' Andreas bravely retorts.

Wisdom is too busy thinking up another word trick to bother retaliating. He is a little shocked that the children have done this well. He has to make it harder for them.

Anita boldly steps forward. 'Go on then Wisdom, try and trick me!'

'Oh you **i**nsolent, **i**gnorant **i**mp', he hisses. 'You think you're so clever, well you're not! I am the only clever one in this room. Try this, you wretched child. If I take the **/t/** away from 'tower' and replace it with **/p/**, what word do I get?'

Ask children to have a go at working this out. Can they make the word 'power'? Try replacing the /er/ with /el/ and see if they can get 'towel'.

Anita lifts her arms and flexes her muscles. 'Power' she says triumphantly. Wisdom falls back in shock. His own power is fading and he is starting to lose control.

The children can see the trap door to the rooftop. They start to climb up to it. Wisdom starts screeching at them.

'You'll never be able to help her, her tragedy is too tragic. You can't possibly change that – not unless you have magic!'

Wisdom's **w**ily **w**ords have given Andreas an idea. It's like a light bulb has just flashed in his brain.

The children get out onto the rooftop where they find Miss Tragic, quivering and quaking in her shoes. She has her hands tied and tears streaming down her face.

The siblings run over to her. Anita quickly assures Miss Tragic.

'Miss Tragic, we have come here to save you'.

Miss Tragic shakes her head. 'You can't possibly help me. I am a tragic tragedy just waiting to happen'.

'It's not true Miss Tragic', Andreas says with great excitement. 'The evil Selves have taught us how to save you without even knowing it. You see, if we make you magical, we can set you free. All we need to do is take the **/tr/** away from 'tragic' and replace it with **/m/** for 'magic'.

tragic – /tr/ = agic + /m/ = magic!

Tragic and magic rhyme so now we can escape just in time! My goodness, I am a poet and I don't even know it. Come on Miss Magic – let's go!'

Wow Andreas is a clever boy! What a team they make.

They escape the tall, towering tower by complete magic and almost immediately end up in their schoolyard.

'Now that I have a new name, I think I might start a new life altogether. My life will no longer be tragic, it will be full of magic and I want to spread my magic as far and wide as possible', *Miss Magic delightfully declares.*

'Yay!' they all shout.

And that is the story

Of how tragic turned to magic.

Thank you and farewell.

Over and out.

Some questions before we finish the book ...

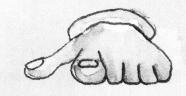

You only need to ask as many questions as you think the child might answer.

Level 4. Can analyse: Can you explain why the children were able to get onto the rooftop?

(Answer: They were able to play against Wisdom's **phonemes** or letter sounds. They could work out his word tricks.)

Level 5. Can evaluate: Which was the hardest word challenge and why?

(Answer: Substituting the sounds from tower to power or tragic to magic. Amazing if the children also notice that the words **rhyme**.)

Level 6. Can create: What word trick could you play on Wisdom? Could you come up with a trick where he would have to play with sounds or **phonemes**?

(Answers will vary.)

Phonological Awareness Games

Here are just a few ideas for practising the different levels of phonological awareness. There are many millions of ideas out there; these are just a start:

Syllables

- **Robot Speaking:** Listen to robot talk on the computer and take in turns to ask each other questions, talking and moving like robots.
- **Tapping/Clapping/Drumming:** Use a musical instrument for beats/syllables in names of friends or family members – listen and say.
- **Syllable Ping-Pong:** Player 1 says syllable first – player 2 says the next one and so on e.g. Adult says 'win' and child says 'dow'.
- **Show Syllables from Picture Cues:** Find pictures of objects, say the names and count the syllables. Winner is the first to count the correct syllables the fastest.
- **Pushing Matchsticks, Counters, Objects Forward:** Use to show the amount of syllables – particularly good if a child has weak working memory (they can count the objects at the end).
- **Identifying Specific Syllables:** e.g. what's the second syllable in com-pu-ter? (pu). Take it in turns to ask each other questions.
- **Deleting Syllables:** e.g. If you take away the 'bit' from 'rabbit' – what are you left with? (rab). Have fun with some of the silly answers.
- **Syllable Bingo:** Find or make a bingo board (or more if playing with more than one child) with six recognisable pictures on them. The pictures should be one, two, three or four syllable words. Provide them with counters or cards to cover the pictures if and when it comes to it. You should have some blank cards with one of the numbers 1–4 written on them. You pick one up, call out a number between 1 and 4 and if the child has a picture with the matching amount of syllables, they can place a counter or card on it. The person who wins will have all their pictures covered.
- **Syllable Snap:** You need at least 20 pictures cards of objects containing 1 to 4 syllables on them. If in a pair, each person should have 10 cards each. They turn over their cards and if the syllables in the name of the picture match, they can say 'snap'. The winner is the person with all the cards at the end. An example would be a card with an elephant (3 syllables) matching a card with a crocodile (3 syllables).

- **Syllable Charades:** A player thinks of a word and tells the other/s how many syllables are in that word. The player then mimes out the meaning of the word. If another player guesses it – it is then their turn to act or mime out their chosen word.

Some words you could use:

One syllable: cat dog house school toy bread class hat

Two syllables: ro-bot pup-pet teach-er mon-key bed-time rain-bow

Three syllables: Sat-ur-day um-brel-la lull-ab-y croc-o-dile cu-cum-ber

Four syllables: hel-ic-op-ter cat-er-pill-ar al-li-ga-tor Jan-u-ar-y cau-li-flow-er

Rhyme

Rhyme detection:

- **Rhyming Pelmanism:** This is also great for training the memory. Make or buy a set of rhyming cards. You probably need around 12 rhyming pairs so 24 cards. Turn them all over so that they are face down. A player picks up two cards and sees if they rhyme. If not, they turn them back over. If a pair matches, the player takes the pair and puts them to one side. The next player does the same thing, trying to remember the place of a rhyming card that might match. The game ends when all the cards have been turned over and the winner is the one with the most pairs.
- **Rhyming Snap:** Make or buy a set of rhyming cards. 12 pairs would suffice or 24 cards. Players take it in turns to turn over their cards. If two cards rhyme, the first player to say 'snap' wins the pair. The winner is the player who ends up with all the cards.
- **Rhyming Bingo:** Find or make a bingo board (or more if playing with more than one child) with six pictures on them. The pictures should each rhyme with a pair that the caller keeps. Provide them with counters or cards to cover the pictures if and when it comes to it. The caller reads out the name of the object on their card, if it rhymes with a picture on the bingo board, the player covers the rhyming picture. The person who wins will have all their pictures covered.
- **Picture and Word:** You will need a selection of words that rhyme with a selection of pictures e.g. 'bar' could rhyme with a picture of a 'car'. The caller reads out a word and the player has to find the matching rhyming picture.
- **Feely Bag:** Find a bag or pillowcase and fill it with pairs of objects that have rhyming names e.g. toy and picture of a boy, hat and toy cat, shell and bell etc.

Players take it in turns to pull out objects and the winner is the one with the most rhyming objects.

- **Odd One Out:** Collect a wide variety of objects, making sure that about two thirds over them rhyme in pairs. Lay three objects in a row and get the other player to find the object that does not rhyme with the other two e.g. a stone, a phone and a shell.

Rhyme generating:

- **Turn-Taking Game:** Try to find a beanbag, soft ball or teddy to throw to each other. Player starts by saying a one-syllable word such as 'dog' and throws the soft object to the next player. When caught, the player has to find a rhyming word such as 'log' and then passes it on. The game ends if a player can't find a rhyming word (give a sensible time limit).

- **Rhyming Cards:** Take it in turns to pick up cards showing one-syllable words. Each player has to think of a rhyming word to match the card. If they get it right, they get to keep the card. The winner is the one with the most cards.

- **I Spy with Semantic Clues:** This is similar to 'I Spy' but you start with something along the lines of: 'I spy something you can drink from that rhymes with 'jug' (mug)'. Players take it in turns.

- **Feely Bag:** Find a bag or a pillowcase and fill it with objects with one-syllable names e.g. toy, phone, bell, sock etc. Players take it in turns to pull out objects and find a word to rhyme with the object e.g. 'shell' rhymes with 'bell'. They can find as many rhyming words, as they want.

- **Rhyming Couplets (poetry):** This is a great one for helping to introduce rhyming verse. Players have to complete the last word of a rhyming couplet e.g. There once was a cat, who slept on a…? (Answer: mat). Have fun finding different versions and extending the couplets into poetry.

Phonemes and Phonemene Awareness

Here are some words you can use for these games. Be careful to remember that some letters combine to make one sound e.g. **/sh/, /ck/, /ow/, /ea/, /igh/, /tch/** etc. A table of phonemes is provided at the end of this section.

2-sound words: i-t, u-s, a-m, u-p, i-f, o-f, sh-e, h-e, m-ay, z-oo, a-t, o-n, n-o, o-ff, wh-y, h-ow, sh-ow

3-sound words: c-a-t, d-o-g, s-u-n, c-u-p, c-a-p, h-a-t, b-i-n, b-u-n, p-e-t, ch-e-ck, m-a-ke, h-ou-se

4-sound words: j-u-m-p, s-t-u-ck, c-r-a-sh, m-i-l-k, d-r-o-p, g-r-ou-p, c-l-a-p, s-t-o-p, t-ea-ch-er

Alliteration:

- **Feely Bag:** Find a bag or a pillowcase and fill it with objects that begin with different sounds. Players take it in turns to pull out objects and they have to find another word that starts with the same sound. You can ask them to find more than one word depending on ability. They then keep the object. The winner is the one who has managed to keep the most objects.
- **Odd One Out:** Present three objects to a player. One of the objects does not start with the same sound as the other two. The player has to identify which one is the odd one out e.g. shell, ship, sock.
- **Turn-Taking:** Try to find a beanbag, soft ball or teddy to throw to each other. Player starts by saying a word and throws it to the next player. That player has to find another word starting with the same sound. The game goes on until they run out of words!
- **I Spy:** One player says 'I spy, with my little eye, something beginning with…' and the other players have to guess what the word is.
- **I Went to the Market:** This is also great as a memory game. A player starts by saying: 'I went to the market and I bought a…' Whatever the object is that they 'bought', the next player has to remember it and then add an object that starts with the same sound. An example could be this, after 5 rounds: 'I went to the market and I bought: a rabbit, a record, a raspberry, a racket and a rose'. This goes on until one of the players forgets the words in their correct order.

Phoneme blending:

- **Counters:** Counters can be used to help count the number of phonemes in a word. One player could say a sound for each counter e.g. /ch/ /a/ /t/ and the other player has to work out what the word is ('chat').
- **Slow-Go:** Players can take it in turns to talk very s-l-ow-l-y asking each other questions, which they have to answer in phonemes e.g. H-ow o-l-d are y-ou? I a-m s-i-x.
- **Uni-Fix Cubes:** Use the cubes to blend individual sounds in words by clicking them together and then saying the whole word. c – u – p – s.
- **Instructions:** Give directions to another player to act out an instruction using phonemes e.g. 'Go to the d-oor and o-p-e-n it'. Take it in turns if you can.

Phoneme segmentation:

- **Board Game:** You will need cards with pictures representing short sounds such as 'mop' or 'rain'. You will also need a simple board for a board game such as a wiggly, winding racetrack. Players take it in turns to pick up the cards and count the amount of phonemes in the word represented by the picture. If they are correct, they move the equivalent number of spaces.
- **Counters or Cubes:** Practise matching counters or cubes to the phonemes in a word. Place the counters down for each phoneme spoken. Picture cards help to give ideas for the words chosen.
- **Aim of the Game:** This will need a bucket and some beanbags or soft toys to throw. A player is presented with a picture card, representing a simple word. They have to count the phonemes and throw a soft object into the bucket for each phoneme. As the game goes on, the words get longer and the bucket can move further away if you want to heighten the competition.

Phoneme deletion:

- **Elision Game:** This is a simple word game where a player asks what a word sounds like once a phoneme is deleted e.g. 'If I took /f/ away from 'fish' – what would I have?' (ish). You can start with the first sound then move on to the end sound e.g. 'If I took /t/ away from 'cat' – what would I have?' (ca).
  Some useful words: bump, clap, drip, shot, tram, clay, blow, brain, slate, clap, spy, pound, plate, bread, flap, shame, hide, slide, track.
- **Counters or Cubes:** You will need counters to represent each phoneme of a chosen word (use picture cards for ideas). A player lays down the counters, whilst saying the word e.g. s-t-o-p (4 counters). Another player takes a counter away and Player 1 has to then say the word that remains e.g. 'top' 'sop' 'stp' 'sto'.
- **What Do I Prefer?** For this game, you need to choose a topic first e.g. colours. You then have to say the colour whilst removing a beginning or an end sound and the other player has to guess what it is. For example; 'I prefer _reen' and the other player would need to guess that it is the colour 'green'. Players take it in turns. Change topics after each player has had a turn.

Phoneme substitution:

- **Guess What I Am Saying:** Choose a favourite nursery rhyme, song, line from a poem or a memorable sentence that would be known to the other players. Each player substitutes sounds for either the beginning or the end of the words e.g.:

Batience is a birtue and birtue is a brace; Brace is a bittle birl who boesn't bosh her bace.

Patience is a virtue and virtue is a grace; Grace is a little girl who doesn't wash her face.

- **Feely Bag:** Find a bag or a pillowcase and fill it with objects that begin with different sounds. Players take it in turns to pull out objects and they have to say the name of the object once they have substituted the first sound e.g. 'doll' could be called 'holl'. Another player has to get guess what that object is and if they are correct, they then keep the object. The winner is the one who has managed to keep the most objects.
- **Picture Cards:** Players take it in turn to pick up cards and say the name of the picture, whilst substituting a sound e.g. 'A jar of honey' might turn to 'a bar of money'. Another player has to guess the picture and they are given three tries at guessing. If they guess correctly, they keep the picture card – if not, the first player keeps their own card.

Phoneme reversals (spoonerisms):

- **Well-Known People:** Players have to choose people that are well known to them and other players (e.g. a member of the family or a teacher in school). There must be two names e.g. Mister Smith or Joe Bloggs. They then swap the first sounds around of the two names. If they are successful with both names, they get 2 points. Successful with one name, they get 1 point. No success is equal to 0 points. An example would be 'Mister Smith' turns to 'Sister Mmith' or 'Joe Bloggs' turns to 'Bloe Joggs'.
- **Name Game:** Players take in turns to say another player's name with a spoonerism. That player then has to do the same so listening skills are required! An example would be; I say 'Holly Mickey' and Molly Hickey would need to say 'Ceorgie Gooney' for me, Georgie Cooney.
- **Compound Words:** There are many compound words you can use to have fun with spoonerisms e.g. 'foot-print' would be 'proot-fint' or 'sun-shine' would be 'shun-sine'. Take it in turns to test one another using some of these words:

pepper-mint	grass-hopper	sun-flower	pan-cake	door-knob	basket-ball	weather-man
back-bone	rail-road	hair-cut	neck-lace	fire-works	grand-mother	grand-father
foot-ball	bed-time	shoe-lace	rattle-snake	pass-port	butter-flies	skate-board

For reference, a list of all the phonemes is given in the table.

VOWEL PHONEMES			
Long vowels		Vowels modified by r	
/ae/	make, maid, stay, weight	/ar/	park
/ee/	feed, beach, scene	/er/	herd, skirt, turn
/ie/	line, fight	/or/	pork, fought, board, hawk
/oa/	stone, goat	/air/	fairy, stare, bear
/ue/	cute, drew	/ear/	hear, cheer
/oo/	spoon, moon		
Short vowels		Diphthong (sound begins as one and moves towards another)	
/a/	hat, cat	/oi/	soil, toy
/e/	egg, bread	/ou/	loud, how
/i/	ink, gym	Schwa (indiscriminate vowel sound)	
/o/	hot, wash	brother, tomato, computer	
/u/	sun, wonder		
/oo/	hood, could		
CONSONANT PHONEMES			
/b/	ball, bubble	/s/	snake, mouse
/c/	cap, kind	/t/	tin, rattle
/d/	dig, muddle	/v/	vet, halve
/f/	fish, physics, stiff	/w/	window, queen
/g/	gate, giggle	/y/	yoghurt
/h/	horse	/z/	zebra, please
/j/	jelly, cabbage	/ch/	chop, catch
/l/	lemon, bell	/sh/	ship, patient, special, mission, sure
/m/	melon, hammer	/th/	their, other
/n/	nose, knot	/th/	thumb
/p/	pig, pepper	/ng/	song
/r/	rabbit, write	/zh/	treasure, vision

T - #0014 - 270324 - C54 - 297/210/3 - PB - 9780367685928 - Gloss Lamination